Uncharted, Unexplored, and Unexplained

Scientific Advancements of the 19th Century

Michael Faraday
and the Discovery of Electromagnetism

Mitchell Lane
PUBLISHERS

P.O. Box 196
Hockessin, Delaware
19707

Uncharted, Unexplored, and Unexplained

Scientific Advancements of the 19th Century

Titles in the Series

Visit us on the web: www.mitchelllane.com
Comments? email us: mitchelllane@mitchelllane.com

Uncharted, Unexplored, and Unexplained

Scientific Advancements of the 19th Century

Michael Faraday
and the Discovery of Electromagnetism

by Susan Zannos

Uncharted, Unexplored, and Unexplained

Scientific Advancements of the 19th Century

Copyright © 2005 by Mitchell Lane Publishers, Inc. All rights reserved. No part of this book may be reproduced without written permission from the publisher. Printed and bound in the United States of America.

Printing   3   4   5   6   7   8   9

Library of Congress Cataloging-in-Publication Data
Zannos, Susan.
    Michael Faraday and the discovery of electromagnetism / Susan Zannos.
        p. cm. — (Uncharted, unexplored & unexplained)
    Includes bibliographical references and index.
    ISBN 1-58415-307-5 (lib. bdg.)
    1. Faraday, Michael, 1791–1867—Juvenile literature. 2. Electromagnetism—History—Juvenile literature. 3. Physicists—Great Britain—Juvenile literature. I. Title. II. Series.
QC16.F2Z36 2005
530'.092—dc22
                                                                    2004002049
ISBN 13: 9781584153078

ABOUT THE AUTHOR: Susan Zannos has been a lifelong educator, having taught at all levels, from preschool to college, in Mexico, Greece, Italy, Russia, and Lithuania, as well as in the United States. She has published a mystery *Trust the Liar* (Walker and Co.) and *Human Types: Essence and the Enneagram* (Samuel Weiser). Her book, *Human Types*, was recently translated into Russian, and in 2003 Susan was invited to tour Russia and lecture about her book. Another book she wrote for young adults, *Careers in Education* (Mitchell Lane) was selected for the New York Public Library's "Books for the Teen Age 2003 List." She has written many books for children, including *Chester Carlson and the Development of Xerography* and *The Life and Times of Ludwig van Beethoven* (Mitchell Lane). When not traveling, Susan lives in the Sierra foothills of Northern California.

PHOTO CREDITS: Cover, pp. 1, 3, 6, 10, 41—Getty/Hulton; pp. 9, 26, 28, 29, 31, 36, 41—Corbis; p. 12—Mary Evans Picture Library; pp. 14, 34—American Institute of Physics; pp. 20, 39—Bridgeman Art Library; pp. 30, 38—Science Photo Library; p. 36—University of Windsor; p. 37—San Francisco State University; p. 40—The Royal Society; p. 40—University of Andrews, Scotland.

PUBLISHER'S NOTE: This story is based on the author's extensive research, which she believes to be accurate. Documentation of such research is contained on page 47.

The internet sites referenced herein were active as of the publication date. Due to the fleeting nature of some web sites, we cannot guarantee they will all be active when you are reading this book.

Uncharted, Unexplored, and Unexplained

Scientific Advancements of the 19th Century

Michael Faraday
and the Discovery of Electromagnetism

*For Your Information

At the age of 21, Michael Faraday became laboratory assistant to Humphry Davy, the brilliant young chemist and lecturer at the Royal Institution of Great Britain. Although he had no formal education, Faraday discovered the laws of electromagnetism and became one of the greatest experimental scientists of all time.

1

A Surprise

The bell of Riebau's Book Bindery rang as a well-dressed gentleman entered.

"Ah, Mr. Dance," George Riebau said, coming from the back of his shop. "Good afternoon to you. Your books are all ready."

Dance looked approvingly at the handsomely bound leather volumes the binder handed to him. "Beautiful work, as always," he said. "How is young Faraday doing? Has he been doing more experiments?"

"Oh yes, his room is full of equipment and contraptions. We got an encyclopedia in for binding, and it had an article on electricity. He's been making one of those voltaic piles. And, here, look at this—Michael wrote these and bound them and dedicated them to me."

The bookbinder handed four neatly bound volumes to his customer. Dance leafed through them with interest. "How extraordinary!" he said. "These are notes from the Tatum lectures, aren't they? Where did the boy learn to draw this well?"

"He's been taking lessons from a French artist who lives upstairs. He cleans the man's room, shines his boots, runs errands for him. I can tell you he really earns his drawing lessons. That Frenchman is a hard master."

Dance smiled. "Not at all like you—I swear you couldn't treat your apprentices better if they were your own sons."

"Well, they're good boys, all three of them, and smart too, but that Michael has a curiosity about everything he sees. I've never seen anything like the way he has to find out how everything works."

"I've brought something for him," Dance said. "Here are tickets for four lectures that Humphry Davy is giving at the Royal Institution. Give them to young Faraday for me, will you?"

"With great pleasure," said Riebau as he wrapped up Dance's newly bound scientific books. "Michael is out delivering some books or you could give them to him yourself and see his joy."

Soon after Dance left the shop, Michael returned. When Riebau handed him the tickets to the Davy lectures, Michael stared at them in amazement. "They're for me? They're really for me?"

He could hardly believe his good fortune. He had seen posters announcing the lecture series given by Davy, who was regarded as the greatest scientist in England. But he had never imagined that he would be able to attend. They were far too expensive for a bookbinder's apprentice. Even his brother Robert, who was a blacksmith and had paid the fee for Michael to attend the Tatum lectures several years earlier, could not have afforded them.

On a cold, damp evening in February 1812, 20-year-old Michael Faraday stood outside the large building at 21 Albemarle Street in the West End of London. This was the Royal Institution of Great Britain. Michael watched the carriages draw up and the finely dressed gentlemen and ladies enter the building. The lecture was a popular event for London society. Humphry Davy was not just a brilliant scientist. He was also a lecturer known for his clear and entertaining presentations. In an age that had no electricity—no movies, no television, no radios, no video or CD players—people went to Davy's lectures for entertainment as much as for knowledge.

The four lectures that Michael Faraday had tickets for were the last in a series of lectures on chemistry that Davy had begun the previous year. Michael sat high up in the lecture hall and took notes on everything Davy said and demonstrated. After each lecture he hurried back to his little room above Riebau's bindery. He didn't sleep until he had carefully copied all of his notes.

In the days that followed he illustrated them with precise drawings of the scientific experiments Davy had demonstrated in his lectures. He carefully bound his notes, drawings, and comments into a book. Michael was an excellent bookbinder. He had learned his craft well.

Humphry Davy was a brilliant chemist and the most popular lecturer at Britain's Royal Institution, one of the most important scientific organizations in the world. In 1813, Davy hired young Michael Faraday to be his laboratory assistant and to accompany him on a scientific tour of Europe.

Even though bookbinding was a steady job and his family needed the money he could earn, Michael didn't want to be a bookbinder. He wanted to be a scientist. The Davy lectures had left no doubt in his mind. Even though he had no formal education, he believed deeply that somehow he had to become a scientist.

His apprenticeship with Riebau ended in October 1812. He quickly got a job as a bookbinder with a man named de la Roche, who had also come to London from his native France. Michael's new employer was

Inspired by the science books he found in Mr. Riebau's bookshop where he was an apprentice, young Michael Faraday began his experiments with electricity. Here Mr. Riebau demonstrates one of the electrical machines to a customer.

harsh and critical. Also, Michael had no joy in his craft. He wrote to a friend that he was "working at my old trade, which I wish to leave at the first convenient opportunity."[1]

He even wrote to the president of the Royal Society, the organization of the best scientists in Britain. He asked for any kind of job in science. He was even willing to be a janitor in a laboratory. His letter was not answered.

Then he had an idea. He would send the book he had made to Sir Humphry Davy himself. He later explained, "My desire to escape from trade, which I thought vicious and selfish, and to enter into the services of Science, which I imagined made its pursuers amiable and liberal, induced me at last to take the bold and simple step of writing to Sir H. Davy expressing my wishes and a hope that, if an opportunity came in his way, he would favour my views: at the same time I sent the notes I had taken of his lectures."[2]

It was a naïve and desperate act. If Michael Faraday had known more about the world, he probably would not have dared to write to such a famous man. Davy, still a young man himself, was impressed with Michael's enthusiasm for science and with the careful notes he had taken at the lecture series. Early in 1813, Davy invited Michael to an interview at the Royal Institution.

Michael was very excited with the prospect of talking with Davy. Unfortunately, after praising the volume of notes and Michael's clear understanding of the principles of chemistry, Davy told the eager young man that there were no positions available at the Royal Institution. He advised Michael to stick with the bookbinding business. "Science is a harsh mistress,"[3] he added.

A few days later, Davy was injured in an explosion during his experiments. Pieces of glass cut his face near his eyes, and he was unable to see to prepare his notes. Again Humphry Davy sent for the young bookbinder. This time he asked Michael to be his secretary and write up his notes while the cuts healed. Michael worked hard and did a good job. In less than a week Davy was able to do his own writing again. Michael was no longer needed.

He was bitterly disappointed. While he was glumly at work binding books for the crabby Mr. de la Roche, fate was arranging quite a surprise for him. William Payne, one of the laboratory assistants at the Royal Institution, had been the subject of several complaints during his 10 years of employment there. About two weeks after Michael had finished helping with Davy's notes, Payne provoked a fight with an instrument maker. They were actually slugging away in the midst of the expensive and delicate instruments in the laboratory. That was the last straw. Payne was fired on the spot.

Davy wrote to the managers of the Royal Institution, "Sir Humphry Davy has the honour to inform the Managers that he has found a person who is desirous to occupy the situation in the Institution lately filled by William Payne. His name is Michael Faraday."[4] Michael was offered a modest salary, with two rooms to live in on the top floor of the Institution.

The Royal Institution of Great Britain was founded in 1799. Its purpose was to provide laboratories for scientific experiments and to present public lectures on scientific knowledge. Michael Faraday spent his entire working life at the Royal Institute and was its most popular lecturer.

Almost exactly a year after he first entered the Royal Institution to hear Davy's lectures, Michael Faraday began his duties as Davy's laboratory assistant. Humphry Davy made many important scientific discoveries during the course of his brilliant career. His most important discovery was Michael Faraday.

Young apprentices learn a trade at a shipyard.

In England during the Middle Ages, craftsmen joined together to form guilds. By the 14th century there were dozens of different guilds in London and other large cities. Each guild regulated particular craftsmen, such as leather workers, goldsmiths, bookbinders, weavers, tailors, bakers, and so forth. The guild rules and regulations were very strict. Anyone not a member of a particular guild could not practice that craft within the territory controlled by the guild. The guilds were the forerunners of modern labor unions.

The first step to becoming a craftsman and a member of a guild was a long apprenticeship. These apprenticeships usually began when a boy was about 14 years old. The boy's parents had to pay his employer to teach him the craft. The employer in turn had to feed, clothe, and provide lodging for the apprentice in exchange for his labor. The nature of the apprenticeship was entirely controlled by the master craftsman. If he was a good and fair man, the system worked well. If he was greedy and unkind, the apprentice could be little more than a slave.

The apprentice was bound to his teacher and employer for about seven years. Then he became a journeyman. This title comes from the French word "jour," which means "day." The journeyman was entitled to be paid daily wages by the master craftsman for whom he worked. After he had worked for several more years, the journeyman could submit his best work to the guild for approval. If his work, or "masterpiece," was accepted, he could join the guild and open his own business.

The guilds controlled the standards of quality in the merchandise that was made and sold by their members. The hours of labor were fixed, and the craftsmen could not work at night or on holidays. Benefits were paid to sick or needy members of the guilds, or to their widows and orphans, so they provided an early form of insurance.

The apprenticeship system is still used today in many trades such as carpentry and electrical work, with the conditions controlled by the unions.

In addition to being one of the greatest scientists of the nineteenth century, Michael Faraday was a kind and deeply religious man who saw no conflict between the Bible and science. He believed that the natural world was God's book just as the Bible was.

2

The Apprentice

Michael Faraday was born on September 22, 1791. His father, James Faraday, had just brought his wife Margaret and their first two children to London. Before that, the Faradays lived in Westmoreland in northern England where James was a blacksmith. Times were hard, and most of the farmers shoed their own horses. The Faradays hoped that James would find more work in London. The family lived for a short while in a suburb, and then moved into a coach house near Manchester Square in London.

Because James Faraday was frequently ill and could not work, the Faradays were very poor. But they were a happy and close-knit family, largely because of their religious faith. They were members of the Sandemanian Church, a small Christian sect that considered itself the only true church. The Sandemanians believed that the Bible was God's word and that it should be followed literally. They attempted to live the way members of the first Christian community had lived. They were not interested in wealth or fame or worldly glory.

When Michael was young, industry was beginning to expand in London and other large cities. Many people, like the Faradays, moved from the country to the cities in hopes of finding work. Many could not find work. Some, like James Faraday, became ill in the polluted city air.

For a while, Michael went to school, but he stayed away from classes so often that he did not get much of an education. He later wrote, "My education was of the most ordinary description, consisting of little more than the rudiments of reading, writing, and arithmetic at a common day school. My hours out of school were passed at home and in the streets."[1] It is a curious fact that one of the greatest scientists who ever lived never learned advanced mathematics.

Before he was old enough to work to help his family, Michael roamed the streets, playing marbles with other boys. When his baby sister was born in 1802, he sometimes took care of her so his mother could work as a maid in rich people's houses to earn a little money. Things got better when his older brother, Robert, was old enough to begin helping his father as a blacksmith.

When Michael was 13 years old he found work with Riebau, a Frenchman who had come to England and established his business in London. Many people in the neighborhood were too poor to buy a newspaper, so they would rent one. Michael's job was to take the newspapers from Riebau's shop to the customers. He returned when the customer had finished reading the paper and took it to the next reader, often covering several miles in the course of a day.

Riebau liked the cheerful and hard-working boy. The Faradays could not afford the usual fee charged when a boy was apprenticed, so Riebau accepted Michael as his apprentice without charging anything. He also provided Michael with a room above the bindery and fed him well.

Riebau had two other apprentices. The three boys enjoyed each other's company and learned quickly from their kindly master. They were like a second family to Michael. Although they learned the trade well, none of the three apprentices would choose bookbinding for a career. Michael became a scientist, one of the other boys became an opera singer, and the third was a comedian in London.

The bookbinding shop provided Michael Faraday's real education. He eagerly read the books that were brought in to be re-bound. He enjoyed them all, but the books about science particularly fascinated him. With Riebau's encouragement, Michael made a small laboratory in his room where he carried out experiments to see if the theories he read about really worked.

In February 1810, Michael heard about John Tatum's lectures. Every other week on Wednesday nights, a group of young men gathered at Tatum's home. They called themselves the City Philosophical Society, and they sponsored Tatum's lectures. The only problem for Michael was that the lectures cost a shilling for each one. He didn't have any money. When he told his brother Robert about it, Robert agreed to pay for 12 lectures. Michael was so grateful for his brother's generosity that he was determined to get every possible benefit from the lectures.

He took sheets of paper stitched in the middle to form a little book. Sitting in the front row, he took notes as rapidly as he could while Tatum lectured, writing down "the most prominent words, short but important sentences, titles of the experiments, names of what subjects came under consideration, and many other hints that would tend to bring what had passed into my mind."[2]

After each lecture, Michael hurried home and immediately began going over the notes he had taken. In the next few nights he wrote up a second and more complete set of notes based on his first ones. He said, "These second set of notes were my guide whilst writing out the lecture in a rough manner. They gave me the order in which the different parts came under consideration and in which the experiments were performed and they called to mind the most important subjects that were dis-cussed. I then referred to memory for the matter belonging to each subject and I believe that I have not let much of the meaning and sense of Mr. Tatum's lectures slip."[3]

In addition to writing out the lectures, Michael made careful drawings of the experiments. If he could devise the proper apparatus, he repeated the experiments in his room at the bindery. He later bound all of his accounts of the Tatum lectures into four volumes, which he dedicated to his employer.

The actual contents were not the only benefit Michael Faraday received from the Tatum lectures. Equally important were the friendships he made with the young men he met there. One of them, Edward Magrath, was highly educated and agreed to help Michael with his writing skills. The two met for weekly study sessions that continued for several years. Another was Benjamin Abbott, a devout Quaker about the same age as Michael. The two agreed to write to each other about their experiments so they would have a written record of their progress. This correspondence lasted for many years and provides a valuable record of Michael Faraday's early development.

Later that year, Michael's father's illness became much worse. On October 30, 1810, James Faraday died. Michael felt an obligation to help support his mother and younger sister. He was good at his work. He knew he could make a good living as a journeyman bookbinder. He would have no trouble becoming a master craftsman and opening his own business. There was only one problem with this pleasant prospect. He didn't want to.

By the time he had the opportunity to hear Davy's four lectures, Michael Faraday knew for certain that he had to be a scientist. When Davy offered him the position of laboratory assistant in 1813, Michael accepted immediately, even though it paid much less than he was earning as a journeyman bookbinder.

Michael's deep religious faith supported his decision. The Sandemanians believed that the Bible was God's word. Michael believed that the book of nature was also God's word. By learning more about the laws of nature, he would discover more about what God had created. Michael Faraday never felt that there was any conflict between his religion and his science. He believed that both his church and his work were ways of serving God.

The Industrial Revolution

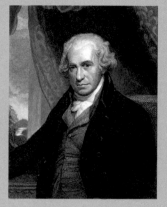

James Watt

By the start of the American Revolution in 1776, another revolution was well under way in England. Known as the Industrial Revolution, it made a greater change in the conditions of human life than any political revolution.

One of the most important inventions that made the Industrial Revolution possible was the steam engine, which was invented early in the 18th century by John Newcomen and significantly improved by James Watt in the late 1760s. Watt and his business partner, industrialist Matthew Boulton, produced nearly 500 engines that powered machinery in many different industries such as pottery, glass, textiles, and many others. As a result of using steam engines, the machinery used in manufacturing processes was no longer dependent on water power, animal power, or human power.

Before the Industrial Revolution began, most people lived in the country and worked in agriculture. Or they lived in small villages and worked in such occupations as blacksmiths, shoemakers, bakers, and tailors. Many of these people began moving to the big cities in hopes of finding work in the factories. By the middle of the 19th century, half of the people in England lived in cities.

The development of railroads—which were also powered by steam engines—made it possible to deliver raw materials to the factories and to send manufactured goods to distant markets. The factories and the railroads created tremendous wealth for their owners. The workers, however, worked long hours for low wages. Many lived in crowded conditions in tenement buildings without proper sanitation. Children of poor families were often forced to work in the factories to help their families survive.

As a result of crowded living conditions and industrial waste from the factories, the air and water around big cities became polluted. Diseases spread among the workers. Because the industrialists were primarily interested in making money, both the workers and the environment suffered.

Only gradually did the governments of industrialized nations begin to pass laws that controlled working conditions. Child labor laws prevented the exploitation of children. Workers organized into unions and went on strike for better working conditions and decent wages. Even now, the struggle to prevent factories from polluting the air and water continues.

Michael Faraday met his devoted wife, Sarah, at the Sandemanian Church they both attended. Although they had no children of their own, they both loved children and their young nieces were frequent visitors in their home at the Royal Institute.

3

The Scientific World

From the beginning of his job at the Royal Institution, Michael Faraday was more than just a laboratory assistant. He worked closely with Davy, who was continuing his work with nitrogen chloride. This was the extremely volatile substance that had caused the explosion that cut his face badly. Michael also experienced several explosions, but he had learned from Davy's accident and wore a mask.

Another project Michael was involved with was extracting sugar from beets. England badly needed a sugar industry that did not depend on imported sugar cane.

Michael was completely involved with his job. He loved it. Humphry Davy, however, was getting restless. He had been at the Royal Institution for 10 years. He enjoyed the fame he received as the Institution's most popular lecturer, but now he wanted new worlds to conquer.

During the previous year, Davy had received a knighthood (and so was now Sir Humphry Davy). This handsome and popular chemist had also broken the hearts of a number of ladies by marrying a wealthy society widow. The new Sir Humphry was ambitious and his new wife Jane was even more so. They decided upon a tour of Europe. Although England and France were at war, Davy received permission from the French emperor Napoleon to travel across France.

Davy invited Michael Faraday to accompany him on the journey as his assistant. Michael agreed, on the condition that he would be guaranteed to get his job at the Royal Institution back when he returned from the trip. At the last minute, Sir Humphry's valet, or serving man, refused to go. Sir Humphry asked Michael to take over the servant's duties until a replacement could be found in Paris. Michael agreed, and they started off on their journey on October 13, 1813. Unfortunately, no replacement for the valet was found.

The journey was quite an experience for Michael. To begin with, he had hardly been outside of his own neighborhood in London in his whole life. He knew nothing of the world, and had not read widely except for his scientific studies. The opportunity to travel in other countries and meet the great scientists of his time was like a miracle to the young man who just a year before had been a penniless bookbinder's apprentice.

On the other hand, Davy's new wife Jane was a nasty and class-conscious woman who treated Michael like a servant. She was constantly ordering him around and criticizing him. Sir Humphry was caught in the middle between his new bride and his assistant. The situation was very unpleasant and made traveling together difficult.

In Paris, Faraday had the opportunity of seeing sugar being extracted from beetroot on an industrial scale. This was a commercial use of the experiments he had been doing at the Institution. Some of their French visitors brought with them a mysterious substance for Davy to experiment with. In their traveling laboratory in their hotel rooms, Davy and Faraday isolated a new element, which they called iodine. They traveled south to the Mediterranean where they analyzed sea-weed to find more iodine.

They crossed the Alps to Italy. In the seaport city of Genoa, they experimented on electric eels, the peculiar fish that can cause an electric shock. In Florence they used the powerful lens used by Galileo to focus the sun's rays for diamond burning, an expensive experiment that proved diamonds were a form of the element carbon. They visited Mt. Vesuvius near Naples and climbed to the top to inspect the volcano. In Pavia they spent time with Alessandro Volta, the greatest living expert in electrical science.

Everywhere they went, Michael Faraday continued his practice of taking detailed notes describing everything he saw and heard. He wrote many letters back to England, primarily to his family and to Benjamin Abbott.

During a three-month holiday in Geneva, Switzerland, Michael met the famous professor of physics, Auguste de la Rive, and began a lifelong friendship with him. When Lady Davy objected to Michael being included in a dinner party, the physicist said that if Michael was not allowed to join them he would have a special party just for him.

They spent the winter months of the following year in Rome, where even the cheerful Michael began to lose patience. He was tired of being treated badly by Lady Davy, and he did not appreciate the great cathedrals and religious art of the Catholics. As a Sandemanian, he believed that simplicity and poverty were required of the true Christian. He missed the companionship of his fellow believers.

Sir Humphry had also tired of the long trip. He had originally planned to continue to Constantinople, Turkey, but instead they returned to England in the summer of 1815. The Michael Faraday who returned to London after nearly two years of travel in Europe was a sophisticated young man. He could read French and Italian. He had done experiments and made important discoveries as Humphry Davy's partner, not just his assistant. He had met and worked with many of the most famous scientists in Europe.

He did not get his old job back at the Royal Institution. Instead he received a promotion. He was made Superintendent of Apparatus and the Mineralogical Collection. His salary was raised by 50 percent, and he was given much better living quarters on the top floor of the Institution. Best of all, he could use any of the laboratories and equipment for his own experiments. Michael's letters to Benjamin Abbott show that he was busy and happy. He spent time with his friends at the City Philosophical Society. He lived near his mother, brother, and sisters and went with them to the Sandemanian Church on Sundays.

Michael Faraday was very sure that he did not want or need a wife. For one thing, he thought that being married would interfere with his scientific studies. For another, his experiences with Humphry Davy's wife had given him a very negative view of marriage. He even wrote a poem on the subject:

> What is the pest and plague of human life?
> And what the curse that often brings a wife?
> 'tis Love.
> What is the power that ruins man's firmest mind?
> What that deceives its host alas too kind?
> What is it that comes in false deceitful guise
> Making dull fools of those that before were wise?
> 'tis Love.[1]

In spite of his dim view of love, however, it wasn't long before he caught the "plague of human life" himself. While attending the Sandemanian Church, he met Sarah Barnard, a silversmith's daughter who was a member of the congregation. Sarah was nine years younger than Michael. He fell completely in love, and gave up his distrust of marriage. Michael courted Sarah with the same energy and determination that he gave to his studies. They were married on June 12, 1821.

A letter that Michael wrote to his young bride shortly after their marriage shows that his attitudes toward love had changed a lot. "Oh, my dear Sarah, poets may strive to describe and artists to delineate the happiness which is felt by two hearts truly and mutually loving each other, but it is beyond their efforts. . . . I have felt it and do feel it, but neither I nor any other man can describe it, nor is it necessary."[2]

Michael Faraday's happy marriage, and the deep religious feeling that he and Sarah shared, formed the foundation for his life and his work.

Charles Dickens

Among the many brilliant artists and writers whom Michael Faraday met in London was the popular novelist, Charles Dickens. Dickens was born in 1812, during the Industrial Revolution. His father, John Dickens, was not good at managing money and was put in debtors' prison when Charles was 12. As the eldest child, he was sent to work at a blacking factory while his parents and the younger children lived in the prison.

The factory work had a terrible psychological effect on the boy. He never completely recovered from his shame and bitterness. After his father was released from prison, his mother thought he should continue working in the factory. Fortunately, his father didn't agree, and sent him to day school in London. When Charles was 15, he had to go to work again. This time it was much more pleasant. In the next few years he worked as an office boy, a shorthand court reporter and then a freelance journalist.

In 1836, he began writing a series of humorous sketches, which were published in regular installments. They were very successful and became his first novel, The Pickwick Papers. In many of Dickens's other novels, a major theme was the sufferings caused by the unjust legal system and the employment of children in factories. Oliver Twist is the story of a boy who is sent to a poor farm and workhouse and later becomes a member of a gang of young thieves. In the autobiographical novel David Copperfield, Dickens used his own experience of working in a factory. In his much-loved story A Christmas Carol, he created the character of Ebenezer Scrooge, a cruel miser whose employees suffer from poverty.

Ebenezer Scrooge

Dickens himself became wealthy and a prominent member of London's high society. He married and had 10 children, but divorced his wife in 1858 and fell in love with an actress soon afterward. At about the same time, he began a series of public readings of his works which were very popular. He had to give those up when his health began to decline. He died of a stroke in 1870.

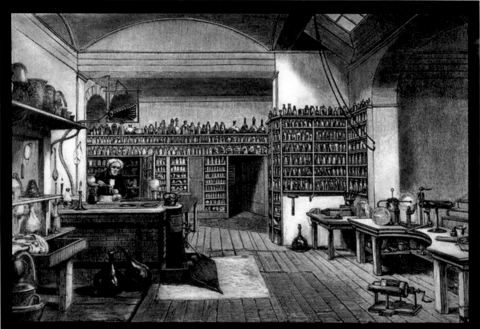

Michael Faraday is shown here at work in his laboratory in Britain's Royal Institution. In 1815 Faraday was appointed Superintendent of Apparatus and the Mineralogical Collection, which entitled him to use any of the laboratories and equipment for his own experiments.

4

The Dynamo

All areas of science interested Michael Faraday. He was endlessly curious about everything he observed. He carried out many different kinds of experiments, but he kept returning to the fascinating phenomenon of electricity. Ever since he had read about electricity in the *Encyclopedia Britannica* when he was still an apprentice bookbinder, he conducted experiments with electricity.

In the same year that Michael Faraday was born, 1791, an Italian biologist named Luigi Galvani made a curious observation. The bodies of dead frogs pinned to metal would twitch when they were touched with another metal. Another Italian, Alessandro Volta, thought the twitching was caused by electricity that was somehow created from the interaction between the two metals and something moist.

To see if his idea was correct, Volta piled up alternating disks made of silver and zinc, placing wet cardboard between them. He then attached a wire to the top disk of silver and the bottom disk of zinc. He was right! An electrical current began to run through the wire. Alessandro Volta had created the first electric battery. It was named the voltaic pile in his honor.

Scientists all over Europe were excited by Volta's experiments. In London, the teenaged Michael Faraday recreated Volta's experiment in

Luigi Galvani (1737–1798) performed experiments demonstrating that electricity could make a frog's leg twitch even when it was removed from the frog. He called this "animal electricity," which paved the way for understanding the electrical impulses of the nervous system.

In 1820, a Danish scientist, Hans Christian Oersted, discovered a connection between magnetism and electricity. He demonstrated that a compass needle (which is a magnet) would point at right angles across a wire conducting an electric current. If the compass was over the wire it would point in one direction, and if under the wire it would point in the other direction. Scientists were fascinated by this

the laboratory he had in his room above the bookbinder's shop. He wrote to his friend Benjamin Abbott, "I, Sir, I my own self, cut out seven discs (of zinc) the size of halfpennies each. I, Sir, covered them with seven halfpences and interposed between seven or six pieces of paper soaked in a solution of muriate of soda."[1] He too was able to produce an electric current.

Later, when traveling in Italy with Sir Humphry, Michael Faraday met Volta. It was one of the highlights of the trip. He was able to spend time with Volta and discuss his experiments. When Michael was back at work at the Royal Institution, it didn't take him long to return to experiments involving electricity.

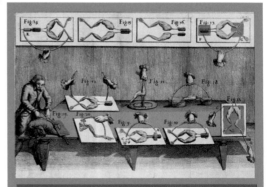

In his laboratory at the University of Bologna in Italy, Luigi Galvani applied static electricity to frogs and other animals, demonstrating that their muscles would contract due to electrical stimulus.

phenomenon and tried to carry out experiments that would reveal the nature of electromagnetism.

In England, a friend of Humphry Davy, William Wollaston, thought that the electric current must travel in a spiral motion down the wire. To prove his theory, Wollaston and Davy carried out experiments at the Royal Institution. They thought that if the theory was correct, a wire carrying a current would turn like a top when brought near a magnet. Their experiments didn't work. The wire didn't turn.

Later the same year, Michael Faraday was asked to write an article about electromagnetism. In his usual thorough way, he reproduced the experiments that had been done by Oersted, Wollaston, and others. In the process,

Italian scientist Alessandro Volta (1745–1827) invented the voltaic pile, the first electrical battery, which produced a steady electrical current. The electrical unit known as the volt was named after him.

he realized that there was a circular force (but not a spiral) created by the electric current. He did an experiment in which a wire circled around and around a fixed magnet, and another in which the wire was fixed and a magnet circled around it. He wrote, "The effort of the wire is always to pass off at a right angle from the pole, indeed to go in a circle around it."[2]

This result was very different from the spiral effect that Wollaston and Davy had looked for but hadn't found. What Faraday had done was, in a very primitive form, create the first electric motor. When he published his paper describing the results in October 1821, he was accused of stealing Wollaston's idea. Wollaston and Davy were both angry. Michael was shocked and hurt by their reaction. He did not return to studying the relationship between electricity and magnetism for several years.

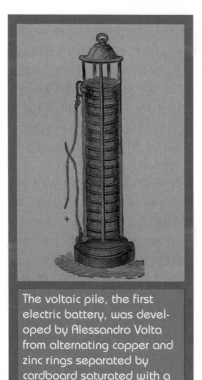

The voltaic pile, the first electric battery, was developed by Alessandro Volta from alternating copper and zinc rings separated by cardboard saturated with a salt solution.

In the meantime, he turned his attention to the process of turning gases such as chlorine into liquids. Humphry Davy was also involved in experimenting with gases. When Faraday published a paper discussing his experiments, Davy once more became angry. He thought Faraday had not given him enough credit. At the same time, in 1823, Michael Faraday was nominated for membership in the Royal Society, the leading scientific organization in England. Davy was president of the organization at that time. He tried to prevent Faraday from being elected as a member.

Faraday's supporters put up a nomination certificate. Faraday later wrote, "Sir H. Davy told me I must take down my certificate. I replied that I had not put it up; that I could not take it down, as it was put up by my proposers. He then said I must get my proposers to take it down. I answered that I knew they would not do so. Then he said, I as President will take it down. I replied that I was sure Sir H. Davy would do what he thought good of the Royal Society."[3]

Probably Davy was jealous of the success and fame Michael Faraday was having. Whatever the reason for his objections, they did no good. Michael Faraday was elected to membership in the Royal Society by all of the members except one.

Faraday finally returned to experiments in electromagnetism in 1831. By that time both Wollaston and Davy had died. Faraday had an important position in the Royal Society as well as his job and experiments at the Royal Institution. Another Englishman, William Sturgeon, had invented the electromagnet by winding a coil of copper wire around a piece of iron. When an electrical current ran through the wire, the iron

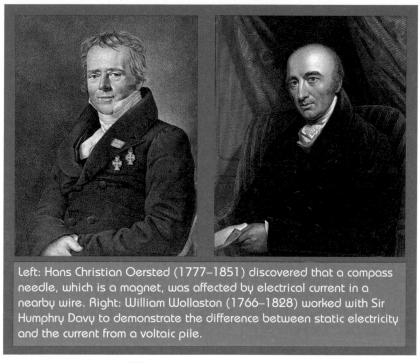

Left: Hans Christian Oersted (1777–1851) discovered that a compass needle, which is a magnet, was affected by electrical current in a nearby wire. Right: William Wollaston (1766–1828) worked with Sir Humphry Davy to demonstrate the difference between static electricity and the current from a voltaic pile.

became a magnet capable of picking up a heavy iron weight. When the current stopped, the iron was no longer magnetic and the weight dropped.

Once again Michael Faraday's curiosity was aroused. There were a lot of unanswered questions about the relationship between electricity and magnetism. If electricity could create a magnetic field, he wondered, could a magnetic field create electricity?

He began to experiment. He coiled two separate wires around an iron ring about six inches in diameter, one on one side and the other on the opposite side. The wires did not touch each other. Faraday connected one of the wires to a battery. He placed a compass underneath a piece of the other wire. When the battery sent an electrical current through the wire it was connected to, the compass under the other wire twitched. When the current was turned off, the compass twitched again. But the needle of the compass only moved when the current was turned on or off. Faraday wanted something that would generate a steady current.

Realizing that some kind of movement was required, Faraday suspended a copper disk between the ends of a strong horseshoe-shaped magnet. One end of a wire connected to the center of the disk, and the other brushed the rim of the disk. When the disk was rotated, a continuous electrical current was generated in the wire. Michael Faraday had proved that magnetism could create electricity! In the process he had created the first dynamo, or electric generator. It was his most impressive accomplishment.

As author John Malone notes, "It would be another half-century before Thomas Edison would begin to light whole cities with large-scale generators constructed on a different model. But the principle on which the new electrified world would be based was established by Michael Faraday on that late October day in 1831."[4]

Shortly after the news of this discovery was published, the British Prime Minister, Sir Robert Peel, visited the Royal Institution. He asked Faraday what use could be made of his electrical discovery. Faraday answered, "I know not, but I wager one day your government will tax it."[5]

Michael Faraday was one of the greatest experimental scientists that ever lived. After his experiments provided the answers to his questions, he had no particular interest in how the results might be used. He left that to the inventors who would come after and develop his ideas into all the electromagnetic technology of the modern world —the appliances that produce light and heat for our homes, the hydroelectric dams and nuclear reactors that produce electricity, the communication networks of telephones and radio and television.

He also had little interest in the theoretical explanations of why his experiments produced their results. One of the reasons was that he did not have the mathematical background to be able to develop his theories. He left this task to theoretical scientists such as James Clerk Maxwell. What Michael Faraday excelled in was the result of his endless curiosity about the world. When something interested and puzzled him, he would not give up until he had devised experiments that would explain the natural laws that governed it. It was his way of learning the way of God's world.

James Clerk Maxwell

James Clerk Maxwell was born in Edinburgh, Scotland on June 13, 1831. He was three months old when Michael Faraday began the experiments demonstrating that a magnetic field could generate electricity. Maxwell would grow up to formulate the mathematical equations that predicted all possible patterns of electromagnetic behavior.

As a child, Maxwell had the same kind of endless curiosity about how things work as Michael Faraday. While Faraday's father was a poor blacksmith, Maxwell's father was a wealthy landowner with an interest in mechanics and science. He gave his brilliant son the best education possible. When James was 10 years old, his father sent him to Edinburgh Academy. Four years later he wrote a paper on the properties of oval curves that was presented to the Royal Society of Edinburgh, the leading scientific organization in Scotland.

When he was 16, James Clerk Maxwell went to Edinburgh University, and later to Cambridge University in England. He did important work in the fields of dynamics, astrophysics, the kinetic theory of gases, and thermodynamics as well as his most significant achievements with electromagnetism.

Inspired by Faraday's experiments which showed that magnets and electrical currents interact with one another, Maxwell was able to map out the interaction of an electrical field on a magnetic field and vice versa. Known as Maxwell's Equations, his findings still are the standard method today of predicting how electricity and magnetism will behave under any conditions.

Maxwell was a different kind of scientist than Faraday. Faraday was an experimental scientist, one who devised specific methods to find out how things work. Maxwell was a theoretical scientist, one who could explain mathematically why things work the way they do. Between the two of them they prepared the way for such inventors as Samuel Morse and the telegraph, Alexander Graham Bell and the telephone, Guglielmo Marconi and the radio, and many others who created the technology of our electronic world.

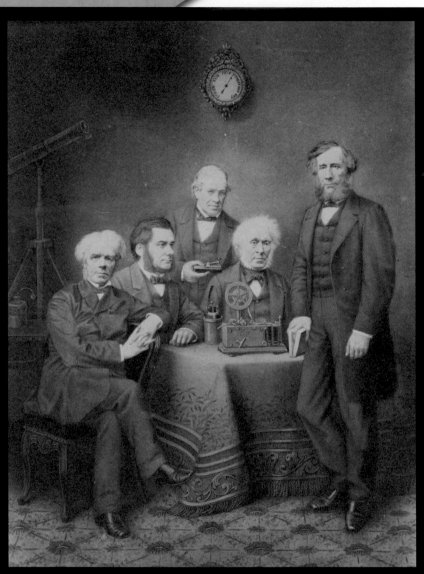

Michael Faraday was acclaimed as one of the greatest scientists of his time. From left to right: Faraday, biologist Thomas Huxley, physicists Sir Charles Wheatley, Sir David Brewster, and John Tyndall. Tyndall became Faraday's assistant at the Royal Institution.

5

A Simple Life

Although Michael Faraday is best known for his work with electro-magnetism, his endless curiosity and careful experiments produced important discoveries in other areas.

His brother Robert left his blacksmithing and found a new job delivering canisters of gas used for heating homes. Robert observed that when the gas was used up, the canisters were not entirely empty. They contained a small amount of thick black liquid. Faraday was, as always, curious. He took some of the liquid and refined it until he had a pure liquid that today is called benzene. It became very important in making dyes, perfumes, and medicines.

Faraday demonstrated that when an electric current passed through certain chemical solutions, they would decompose. As a result of these experiments he discovered the process of electroplating, which is coating one metal with another. With this process, for example, an ordinary iron candleholder can be covered with a thin layer of gold so it looks as shiny and expensive as if it were solid gold. Or metal spoons can be covered with a coat of silver.

As a result of his many important discoveries, in 1825 Faraday became Director of the Laboratory at the Royal Institution. Eight years

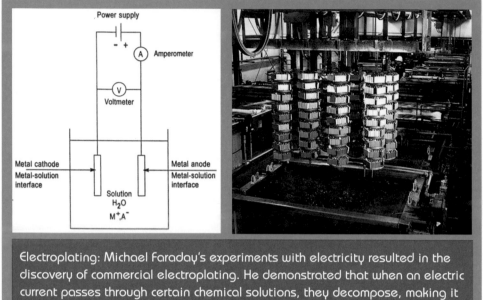

Electroplating: Michael Faraday's experiments with electricity resulted in the discovery of commercial electroplating. He demonstrated that when an electric current passes through certain chemical solutions, they decompose, making it possible to coat one metal with another.

later he was appointed as Fullerian Professor of Chemistry there. His duties included arranging lectures on scientific topics, some of which he gave himself. As with everything he did, he approached the art of lecturing by studying it seriously. He wrote that a lecturer's "whole behavior should evince a respect for his audience, and he should in no case forget that he is in their presence . . . he should never, if possible, turn his back to them."[1]

Faraday became an even more popular lecturer than Humphry Davy had been. The Friday Evening Discourses, as they were called, were among the most important functions of the Royal Institution. They are still given today.

Faraday gave more than a thousand lectures, covering a wide range of topics. These included "Silicified Plants and Fossils," "Early Arts: The Bow and Arrow," "The Atmosphere of This and of Other Planets," "Plumbago and the Manufacture of Pencils from it with Modern Machinery," and, of course, many lectures on various aspects of electricity and magnetism. In addition, he arranged for other major scientists to present their research findings at the Royal Institution.

It didn't take him long to reach out to a new audience. In 1826 he began a series of Christmas Lectures for Children. His most famous one was entitled "The Chemical History of a Candle." He would darken the auditorium and light a candle. Then he would ask questions about the candle. What was it made of? Why was the flame brightest at the top? Why did it go out if it was placed in a

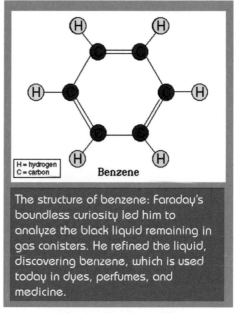

H = hydrogen
C = carbon

Benzene

The structure of benzene: Faraday's boundless curiosity led him to analyze the black liquid remaining in gas canisters. He refined the liquid, discovering benzene, which is used today in dyes, perfumes, and medicine.

glass jar? Then he would answer the questions he had asked. This lecture was so popular with the children that he repeated it every year.

The children liked Faraday's lectures so much that they would gather in the street where they knew he would pass by on his way to church so they could greet him. This pleased him because he liked children so much. These lectures for children are just as popular today and remain an important part of the Royal Institution's traditions. They are given every year on television, too.

It is widely accepted that Faraday was a kind and gentle man. His assistant John Tyndall, the man who followed him as the head of the Royal Institution, observed, "Underneath his sweetness and gentleness was the heat of a volcano. He was a man of excitable and fiery nature; but through high self-discipline he had converted the fire into a central glow and motive power of life, instead of permitting it to waste itself in useless passion."[2]

Although Michael Faraday became the most respected and famous scientist in Great Britain, he continued to live a simple private life. He and his beloved wife Sarah lived in their apartment on the top floor of

John Tyndall (1820–1893) was an Irish physicist who became Michael Faraday's assistant and later succeeded him as head of the Royal Institution.

the Royal Institution. They didn't have children, which was a sorrow for them, but they enjoyed the company of their nieces and nephews who often visited. Two of their nieces lived with them for a while.

True to the beliefs of his religion, which rejected wealth and fame, Faraday refused many of the honors that he was offered. In 1827 he was offered the position of professor of chemistry in a new university being established in London. He rejected the offer, even though he was promised new laboratories and complete research freedom. He said that he owed a great deal to the Royal Institution and would not leave now that he was successful. In his later years Michael Faraday refused the honor of a knighthood, and twice refused the presidency of the Royal Society.

In spite of his refusal to accept fancy titles, universities and scientific institutions all over the world honored him with gold medals and honorary diplomas. The medals did not impress him—he just tossed them into a box. But he was proud of the honorary diplomas. They were evidence that he had by himself achieved the education he had not been able to afford when he was a young man.

As he aged, Faraday's memory began to fail him. Modern biographers suspect that that he "was suffering from mercury poisoning; in electric connections he made great use of cups of mercury, some of which would, no doubt, be spilt occasionally on the floor of the laboratory and ultimately vaporized."[3]

Faraday became more and more depressed and withdrawn as he realized his memory was getting worse. When he was 50 years old, he suffered a nervous breakdown. His doctor told him that he had to have complete rest and not think about his scientific work. His wife nursed him and protected him from people who wanted to talk to him about his ideas. The two of them went to the theater, and to the zoo, and took trips to the country. Gradually, Michael Faraday's health improved enough so that he could continue to work. But his loss of memory made it necessary for him to write down everything he observed.

Faraday's induction coil consists of two separate wires coiled around an iron ring about six inches in diameter, one on each side, not touching each other. When Faraday sent an electrical current through one wire, a compass under the other wire moved.

Eventually he had to give up the activities he had performed for half a century. In 1860 he wrote, "My memory wearies me greatly in working; for I cannot remember from day to day the conclusions I come to. . . . I do not remember the order of things, or even the facts themselves."[4]

His problems were physical as well as mental. When it became clear that it was difficult for him to climb the stairs to the apartment on the top floor of the Royal Institution, Queen Victoria provided him with a home at Hampton Court. The queen even paid for fixing the house up when she realized the Faradays could not afford to do so.

Michael Faraday gave his last Christmas lecture to the children in 1861, and his last Friday Night Discourse the following year. In 1864 he resigned as an elder in the Sandemanian church. The following year he resigned from the Royal Institution. On August 25, 1867, he died peacefully while sitting in his study in the house at Hampton Court.

Not all of Michael Faraday's ideas were accepted during his lifetime. He did not agree with the scientists of his time who believed atoms were the smallest units possible. His belief in electrons and how they

This silver gilt medal is the Royal Society Michael Faraday Prize, which is awarded annually to the scientist or engineer who best communicates scientific ideas to the public.

function was too advanced for his time. Other scientists rejected his theory about the unity of energy and matter. They thought he was crazy when he said that light could be affected by magnetism.

Not until the 20th century did the noted scientist Albert Einstein prove, during an eclipse of the sun, that the force of the sun's gravity bends light rays. Faraday had demonstrated the same thing 70 years before, but no one then would listen to him.

As a tribute to his contributions to science, Michael Faraday has the unusual honor of having two units named for him. One is the faraday, a measurement of electrical charge in certain substances. The other is the farad, which measures electrical capacity.

Because he was one of Britain's greatest scientists, Michael Faraday's picture was featured on England's 20 pound note. The pound has been replaced by the euro as Britain's currency.

This plaque can be seen on the building that housed Riebau's Book Shop where Michael Faraday spent his youth as an apprentice book binder. It was here that his earliest experiments in electricity were performed.

The Royal Institution of Great Britain became one of the most respected scientific institutions in the world under the leadership of Michael Faraday in the 19th Century. Faraday's lectures for children started a tradition that has continued until this day. The lectures are now televised.

On March 7, 1799, the Royal Institution of Great Britain had its first meeting. It was the brainchild of Count Rumford, a British nobleman who was born as Benjamin on an American farm in 1753. A British loyalist who fled to England when the American Revolution broke out, he was knighted by King George III and later became a Count of the Holy Roman Empire.

He was also a scientist and sociologist who had many projects. One was the Society for Bettering the Condition and Increasing the Comforts of the Poor. After failing to make the poor more comfortable, Count Rumford turned his attention to starting a new public institution, which would provide both a site for research and inventions and offer public presentations about how scientific knowledge affected the daily lives of people.

Michael Faraday lecturing

This was the Royal Institution, which Rumford co-founded with Sir Joseph Banks, president of the Royal Society of London. In addition to gaining the support of Sir Joseph, Count Rumford convinced Humphry Davy to lecture in chemistry and direct the laboratory. Davy's lectures attracted the most wealthy and influential members of London society. The lectures became so popular that Albemarle Street—where the Royal Institution is still located—was jammed with carriages. The only way to control the traffic was to make it London's first one-way street.

More than 200 years later, over 60 scientists are either studying or doing research in the laboratories of the Royal Institution in preparation for becoming professors. Besides being an important research facility, Davy's heritage continues as the Royal Institution continues to inform the public about the scientific developments that affect daily life. In addition to adults, more than 30,000 children attend lectures about scientific topics every year. Countless thousands view the televised programs that the Royal Institution presents.

Chronology

1791	Born on September 22 in London
1802	Sister Margaret born
1804	Finds work as errand boy for bookbinder George Riebau
1805	Is accepted as Riebau's apprentice
1810	Attends the Tatum lectures and binds his notes into books; father James dies
1812	Attends Humphry Davy's chemistry lectures
1813	Appointed laboratory assistant at the Royal Institution; tours Europe with Humphry Davy and his wife Jane
1815	Returns to Royal Institution as superintendent of apparatus
1816	Gives his first lecture at the Royal Institution
1821	Marries Sarah Barnard; conducts first experiments on electromagnetism
1823	Liquifies gases; elected to membership of Royal Society
1825	Discovers benzene; becomes director of laboratory at the Royal Institution
1831	Generates electricity with magnetic field
1833	Discovers laws of electrolysis
1840	Appointed elder of Sandemanian Church
1857	Refuses presidency of Royal Society
1858	Given house at Hampton Court by Queen Victoria
1861	Resigns from Royal Institution
1867	Dies on August 25

Timeline of Discovery

1746	Pieter van Musschenbroek invents the Leyden jar, which stores static electricity.
1747	Benjamin Franklin experiments with static charges in the air; Henry Cavendish measures the conductivity of different materials.
1752	Benjamin Franklin invents the lightning rod.
1767	Joseph Priestley discovers that electricity follows Newton's law of gravity.
1786	Luigi Galvani makes frog muscles jump with electricity, demonstrating the electrical basis of nerve impulses.
1800	Alessandro Volta makes the first electric battery.
1820	Hans Christian Oersted discovers the magnetic field around an electric wire; Francois Arago invents the electromagnet.
1830	Joseph Henry sends an electrical current over a mile of wire, which becomes the principle of the telegraph.
1837	Electric motors are used for industrial purposes for the first time.
1873	James Clerk Maxwell writes equations describing electromagnetic field and predicts electromagnetic waves traveling at speed of light
1876	Alexander Graham Bell invents the telephone.
1879	Thomas Edison demonstrates the incandescent light bulb.
1881	In Niagara Falls, a brush dynamo connected to an electric turbine provides energy to light street lamps.
1887	Heinrich Hertz devises an experiment to prove Clerk Maxwell's theory.
1888	Nikola Tesla invents rotating field AC alternator.
1897	J.J. Thomson discovers the electron.
1907	Lee DeForest invents the electronic amplifier.
1910	Robert Millikan publishes the first results of his measurements of the electric charge on a single electron.
1947	Bell Telephone Laboratories scientists John Bardeen, Walter Brattain, and William Shockley invent the transistor.
1950	There are 10 million television sets and 90 million radios (two per home) in U.S. homes.
1957	The Soviet Union launches *Sputnik 1*, the first earth satellite, which transmits radio signals back to earth.
1961	The Federal Communications Commission (FCC) authorizes FM stereo broadcasting.
1962	Telstar satellite transmits video images across the Atlantic Ocean.
1984	The first North American tidal power plant opens in Nova Scotia, Canada.
1986	An accident at the Chernobyl nuclear power plant in the Soviet Union kills dozens of people and releases large amounts of radiation.
1997	Mars *Pathfinder* spacecraft lands on Mars and beams images back to earth.
1999	Electric companies use the internet to market electricity.
2003	Astronomers break ground on the site of the world's largest radio telescope, located on land donated by the government of Chile.
2004	Forty-nine countries have agreed to participate in a 10-year project to collect and share thousands of measurements of the Earth.

44

Chapter Notes

Chapter 1   A Surprise
1. John Gribbin and Mary Gribbin, *Faraday in 90 Minutes* (London: Constable & Co. Ltd., 1997), p 20.
2. John Meurig Thomas, *Michael Faraday and the Royal Institution* (London: Adam Hilger, 1991), p. 17.
3. Ibid.
4. Charles Paul May, *Michael Faraday and the Electric Dynamo* (New York: Franklin Watts, Inc., 1961), p. 44.
The dialogue in this chapter represents the author's interpretation of what might have happened, based on her extensive research, and is solely an aid to readability.

Chapter 2   The Apprentice
1. Colin A. Russell, *Michael Faraday: Physics and Faith* (New York: Oxford University Press, 2000), p. 22.
2. Charles Ludwig, *Michael Faraday, Father of Electronics* (Scottdale, PA: Herald Press, 1978), p. 85.
3. Ibid.

Chapter 3   The Scientific World
1. Colin A. Russell, *Michael Faraday: Physics and Faith* (New York: Oxford University Press, 2000), p. 44.
2. Ibid.

Chapter 4   The Dynamo
1. John Meurig Thomas, *Michael Faraday and the Royal Institution* (London: Adam Hilger, 1991), p. 16.
2. John Gribbin and Mary Gribbin, *Faraday in 90 Minutes* (London: Constable & Co. Ltd., 1997), pp. 29-30.
3. Colin A. Russell, *Michael Faraday: Physics and Faith* (New York: Oxford University Press, 2000), p. 66.
4. John Malone, *It Doesn't Take a Rocket Scientist: Great Amateurs of Science* (Hoboken, NJ: John Wiley & Sons, Inc., 2002), p. 110.
5. Ibid., p. 90.

Chapter 5   A Simple Life
1. Stewart Ross, *Michael Faraday* (New York: Raintree Steck-Vaughn Publishers, 2003), p. 27.
2. John Meurig Thomas, *Michael Faraday and the Royal Institution* (London: Adam Hilger, 1991), p. 117.
3. D.K.C MacDonald, *Faraday, Maxwell, and Kelvin* (Garden City, NY: Anchor Books, 1964), p. 45.
4. Ross, *Michael Faraday*, p. 38.

Glossary

apparatus (ap-puh-RAT-us)—the tools and materials needed for a task.

apprentice (uh-PRENT-us)—a young person working with a craftsman to learn a trade.

canister (CAN-uh-stur)—a metal container.

chemistry (KEM-uh-stree)—the study of the composition of matter.

compass (KUM-pus)—an instrument with a magnetic needle that indicates direction.

conductor (kun-DUK-ter)—a material that allows the passage of an electric current.

current (KURR-unt)—a stream of electrons moving through a conductor.

dynamo (DYE-nuh-moe)—a machine that changes mechanical energy to electricity.

electromagnet (ee-lek-troe-MAG-nut)—a device in which magnetism is created by an electric current.

electroplating (ee-lek-troe-PLAY-ting)—a process in which a thin layer of metal is applied to the surface of a metal object.

magnetism (MAG-nuh-tizm)—the force that attracts or repels metal objects.

pole (POHL)—one end of a magnet.

Sandemanians (san-duh-MAYN-ee-uns)—members of a Christian church founded in Scotland.

valet (val-LAY)—a personal manservant.

volatile (VOL-uh-tul)—changing to a gas quickly at ordinary temperatures.

voltaic pile (vol-TAY-ick pile)—the first battery, composed of alternating disks of metal with moist cardboard between the disks.

For Further Reading

For Young Adults

Brophy, Michael. *Michael Faraday.* New York: The Bookwright Press, 1991.

Fullick, Ann. *Michael Faraday.* Chicago: Heinemann Library, 2001.

Gutnik, Martin J. *Michael Faraday, Creative Scientist.* Chicago: Children's Press, 1986.

Harvey, Tad. *The Quest of Michael Faraday.* Garden City, NY: Garden City Books, 1961.

Ludwig, Charles. *Michael Faraday, Father of Electronics.* Scottdale, PA: Herald Press, 1978.

Ross, Stewart. *Michael Faraday.* New York: Raintree Steck-Vaught Publishers, 2003.

Veglahn, Nancy. *Coils, Magnets, and Rings: Michael Faraday's World.* New York: Coward, McCann & Geoghegan, Inc., 1976.

Works Consulted

Gribbin, John and Mary Gribbin. *Faraday in 90 Minutes.* London: Constable & Co. Ltd., 1997.

MacDonald, D.K.C. *Faraday, Maxwell, and Kelvin.* Garden City, NY: Anchor Books, 1964.

Malone, John. *It Doesn't Take a Rocket Scientist: Great Amateurs of Science.* Hoboken, NJ: John Wiley & Sons, Inc., 2002.

May, Charles Paul. *Michael Faraday and the Electric Dynamo.* New York: Franklin Watts, Inc., 1961.

Russell, Colin A. *Michael Faraday: Physics and Faith.* New York: Oxford University Press, 2000.

Thomas, John Meurig. *Michael Faraday and the Royal Institution.* London: Adam Hilger, 1991.

On the Internet

Michael Faraday (1791–1867)
http://home.att.net/~newtuniv/faraday.html

Michael Faraday
http://www.spartacus.schoolnet.co.uk/SCFaraday.htm

The Royal Institution of Great Britain: Heritage Faraday Page
http://rigb.org/heritage/faradaypage.html

Charles Dickens
http://www.incwell.com/Biographies/Dickens.html

The Royal Institution of Great Britain
http://www.rigb.org

Modern History Sourcebook: Michael Faraday: The Chemical History of a Candle
http://www.fordham.edu/halsall/mod/1860Faraday-candle.html

Index